a new
ir and
vigour

r first

s with
Times

Another book by Jackie Kay

TWO'S COMPANY

THREE
HAS
GONE

Poems by
Jackie Kay

Illustrated by
Jody Winger

PUFFIN BOOKS

PUFFIN BOOKS

Published by the Penguin Group
Penguin Books Ltd, 27 Wrights Lane, London W8 5TZ, England
Penguin Books USA Inc., 375 Hudson Street, New York, New York 10014, USA
Penguin Books Australia Ltd, Ringwood, Victoria, Australia
Penguin Books Canada Ltd, 10 Alcorn Avenue, Toronto, Ontario, Canada M4V 3B2
Penguin Books (NZ) Ltd, 182–190 Wairau Road, Auckland 10, New Zealand

Penguin Books Ltd, Registered Offices: Harmondsworth, Middlesex, England

First published by Blackie 1994
Published in Puffin Books 1996
1 3 5 7 9 10 8 6 4 2

Filmset in Plantin

Made and printed in England by Clays Ltd, St Ives plc

For my father, John Kay

Contents

The Stincher

When I was three, I told a lie.
To this day that lie is a worry.

Some lies are too big to swallow;
some lies so gigantic they grow

in the dark, ballooning and blossoming;
some lies tell lies and flower,

hyacinths; some develop extra tongues,
purple and thick. This lie went wrong.

I told my parents my brother drowned.
I watched my mother chase my brother's name,

saw her comb the banks with her fingers
down by the river Stincher.

I chucked a stone into the deep brown water,
drowned it in laughter; my father, puffing,

found my brother's fishing reel and stool
down by the river Stincher.

I believed in the word disaster.
Lies make things happen, swell, seed, swarm.

Years from that away-from-home lie,
I don't know why I made my brother die.

I shrug my shoulders, when asked, raise my
eyebrows: *I don't know, right, I was three*.

Now I'm thirty-three. That day they rushed me
to the family friends' where my brother sat

undrowned, not frothing at the mouth, sat
innocent, quiet, watching the colourful TV.

Outside, the big mouth of the river Stincher
pursed its lips, sulked and ran away.

Bull

Once, so I am told,
I was chased by a bull.
I was three years old.
I ran fast as a Ferrari,
so I am told,
across the big field.
Then I got to the fence
a split second before,
so I am told,
the big bull got there;
it was about to ram me
with its active angry horns,
so I am told,
but I climbed through
a hole in the barbed wire
breathing faster than Dracula,
so I am told.
I jumped into the arms of my mother
who kissed my cheeks a hundred times,
said my name a hundred times, like this,
so I am told –
Aw Joooooooooaaaaaannnnnne Joooooooaaannnne . . .
I don't remember any of it.
Don't remember waving the red hanky.
Lucky for me,
so I am told.

Four:Eight Time

An hour is down my road, and down the other, and
  back.
Is the length of a giant's face.
An hour is from here to that mirror.
Bravo! An hour is about twelve eggs.

Ten minutes is just around the corner,
or from here to that woman in red.
Ten minutes is the length of my leg.
Hotdog! Ten minutes is an icecream cone.

One minute is a flash of lightning,
or my balloon bursting; me tripping on my laces.
One second is the length of my pinky finger.
Yippee! One second could disappear.

Things of the Past

I liked being a baby a lot better,
not having to bother with words.
I remember opening my mouth
and sounds flying out like strange birds.
The comfort of talcum powder on a clean bottom.
Not having to trouble myself with zips and flushes.
Or reading. Or doing sums.
I just sat, fat, and everything was done.
I was fed by two comfy pillow breasts.
Or later, the spoon. I even got to throw
my food on the floor, smash eggs
from the fridge. Scream.

I'd never get away with all that, now
that I am eight, I've got to do things I hate
like make my own bed. When I was a baby
nobody would have thought
of asking me to make my cot.
Or dragged me along the street.
In my buggy, I put up my feet,
sucked my dummy, had a sleep.
But all that's a thing of the past.
When I'm eighteen will I be wishing
I was stuck at the top of the climbing-frame?
I'll just have to accept it:
children grow up; things change.

Charles Dickens and the Dinosaurs

When Charles Dickens was writing Dombey
and Son, Diplodocus was running
(all twenty-six point six metres of her)
past his window at a furious speed;
a gentle giant hungry for plants.
People have it easier these days.
Then, people lived in bleak houses,
huddled together in the same room.
Diseases spread very quickly:
brachiosaurus caught bronchitis;
His cough threw David Copperfield
into the following week. His mututal friend
T rex caught TB and couldn't catch live prey.
The Dodger couldn't pickpocket enough money.
Times were hard, especially at Christmas
when all the dinosaurs, meat-eaters and veggies,
joined together to sing a Christmas Carol
for a little boy who was dying. People
marvelled at the sound of the dinosaurs singing.
All this happened when Dickens lived,
a very long time ago, in the age of the dinosaurs.
But the poor are always with us.

The School Hamster's Holiday

Remember the coal bunker in winter?
Naw? You wouldn't want to, either.
Stooping at the grate gathering auld ash.

Always leaving a wee bed of ash
for the next fire's blazing dreams.
Heeking a' that heavy coal from the bunker.

The big black jewels in the steel bucket.
Toast from the naked flame was a treat,
or burning pink and white marshmallows

till they caved in and surrendered.
But that was rare.
This is what I most remember:

The time when Snowie, our school hamster,
came home for a weekend holiday with me.
A cage is a cage no matter where the house is,

thinks Snowie, probably, so come nighttime
she escapes her prison, come nighttime
she fancies a night in a Slumberdown,

climbs up the chimney breast
into the ma and the da's bed.
You should have heard them scream

when they woke to see Snowie,
now the colour of soot, no snaw,
running the course of the duvet.

They were big screams like this:
AAAAAAAAAAAAAAAAAAAAAAAAAAAAAA
AAAAAAAAAAAAAAAAAAHHHHHHHHHHHH

I spent the rest of the weekend
tight-lipped and desperate,
sponging that hamster with all my might

my wee yellow sponge going like a wiper,
hearing children chant in my ears,
She's made our Snowie into a darkie.

I tried and tried to make Snowie white.
It wis an impossible task.
Have you ever tried to shammy a hammy?

Monday morning wis an absolute disgrace.
I'll never forget the shame of it.
The wee GREY hamster looking po-faced.

Outdoor Pool

My father shows us the place
in the middle of the Carbeth hills
that used to be a swimming pool,
an open-air swimming pool.
'Me and Spanner and Goldie
came as boys, walked the seven mile
then swam. All this part here.'
He points to a cavity of mud
where workmen in yellow boots
practise demolition. 'All this
used to be packed, us drying
on the hill after our swim.'
He walks fast as he can,
his one arthritic hip
making him lopsided, but faster
than his grandson trailing in oversized wellies,
shouting, 'Swimming pool? swimming pool?
You must be mad, Grandpa.'

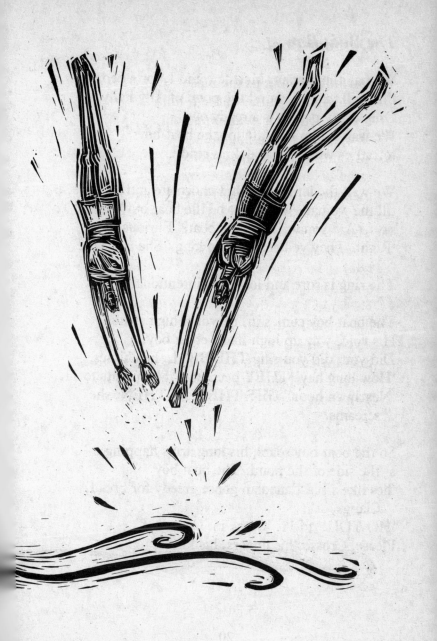

The Boat Boy

We pay the money, Matthew and I, for a pedalo
that will take us round the pond of Ally Pally.
Only every pedalo is already out.
We wait in the sad café for the boat boy
to call us when the pedalo is ready.

We wait the length of a hot chocolate and a coffee,
till the woman, who must be the boat boy's boss,
says, 'Are you waiting on a boat?' Furious.
'Right. They've been out too long.' She rings the
    bell.
The ring is sore and long and intentional.

The boat boy comes in, nervous, high strung.
His voice way up high like a choir boy.
Did you, did you ring THE BELL, he chimes.
'How long have THEY been out?' She points to 11.
'Nearly an hour.' GET THEM IN THEN, she
    screams.

So the boat boy soars, his long arms flapping
at the side of the pond. The boat boy
flies like a big Canadian goose greedy for bread.
    Clangs,
'HO YOU!' to 11. 'Come in. Come in.'
Please. Crosses his fingers, his knees.

11 ignore him. Their laughter ripples the water.
They chase the ducks. Splash the clothes of 10.
Jump out at the island that says KEEP OFF.
Till finally the boat boy, sweating, shouts:
Pleeeeeeeeeeeeeeeease. Spinning his voice in the air.

It travels fast as a frisbee and hits their ears.
11 leave the island. Pedal slowly in.
Matthew and I hop in our boat.
The boat boy grimaces. We pedal pell-mell.
'She makes me nervous when she rings her bell.'

De-icing the Pond

The first day in winter we go down
to the pond at Clissold Park, it is so sad
because none of the ducks can get their food.
But I can't help myself laughing
at the way the webbed feet skid on the ice
like drunk ducks, ducks running a high fever,

or, more like ducks doing the moonwalk.

The next day is so cold the car window is ice.
My mum gets a green bottle from her boot,
sprays it on the window till the ice melts. Magic.
She calls the special bottle *de-icer*.
I don't go to the pond this day.
I know it will horrify me, those hungry ducks.

The night after, I have a fantastic idea.
I wake my mum up shouting, *de-icer*.
de-icer de-icer. She thinks I've lost
my marbles, till I let her into my mind.
In no time we're down in the dark at the park,
with two massive green bottles, size of trees.

We float over the pond with our magic bottle
We watch the ice melt like a frown on a cross face.
We keep spraying till we hear the first duck
  splashing.
Then throw in our midnight bread for good
  measure.
After, we're so exhausted we look like
we're drunk with tiredness walking back to the car,

or more like *we're* doing the moonwalk.

Blue Slip

She remembers, once, getting to wear
her sister's, Maisie's, new jacket;
she remembers taking a walk in it,
loving the wide furry hood, the big zip.
She remembers passing a sign that said
Don't stray from the Path,
and because it annoyed her when someone said
   DON'T,
she remembers thinking she would.

Four hours later, she remembers, Maisie waiting
under the old apple tree with a slice of malice
cut across her cheek – *Where have you been?*
Then, she remembers, Maisie seeing
the favoured jacket covered in blue slip,
Maisie's loud and demanding screams,
the tears pouring down both faces,
My new jacket. My new jacket.

Two hours it had taken her to walk
the length of a house, gingerly stepping
on something that looked like a punk's hair,
then sinking so fast into the quick, greedy mud.
She had clung to the held-out hand of a branch,
an olive branch, as if she were at war with the sand.
Finally, she held on to *barbed wire*
all the way back to her sister

Who was now standing under
the apple tree shouting *How could you*.
She didn't get a chance to say
I nearly died. Nothing mattered
but that the new hood was full of blue slip,
the new zip didn't work. And the sleeves,
when you squeezed them, belched.
Look, Maisie screamed, *look at my zip*.

Grange-over-Sands

I was all set to play with my whooosh
when I saw a sign that said,
QUICKSAND: IF IN TROUBLE CALL 999.
Every time I tried to get down to the beach
this message reappeared like a boomerang,
QUICKSAND: IF IN TROUBLE CALL 999.
I walked along the promenade
and passed this message several times,
QUICKSAND: IF IN TROUBLE CALL 999.

I held my whoosh limp at my wrist
and puzzled over this message.
Imagine sinking by the minute
sinking so fast your shoes go first
then your trousers, then all of a sudden
the quicksand has touched your shoulders,
how *on earth*, especially on sinking earth,
would you manage to call 999?
If you did would they get there in time?

Would there be a batphone at the bottom
or would you need a mobile phone?
Imagine when dialling your second 9
your phone sinks for all time.
I decided to give my whoosh a miss.
I asked a woman if anywhere was safe,
pointing to the big 999 sign.
'No,' she sighed, 'it's always
been muddy has Grange-over-Sands.'

Dial L for Lightning

Tonight my telephone was struck by lightning.
A roll of thunder somersaulted
the numbers nothing to nine.
Hit this button ✻ and this #
I've got something to tell Charlene
but my telephone has been struck by lightning.

The line that the pigeons perch on is dead.
The chat that tickled their feet is mute.
My telephone has had a nervous breakdown.
It won't talk to anyone or let anyone talk to it.
It used to say MMMMMMMMMMMMMMMM.
Now it says nothing. A crackle of a mad laugh.

I've watched everyone hang up, crack up, shut up.
Hit the receiver on the wall. Twist the ear.
Breathe into the mouth. Push the button up, down,
    sideways.
Finally when no one is near by I talk to her anyway:
I won't let a dead line stop me. 'Charlene?' I say
to the calm after the storm, 'You'll never guess
    what . . .'

The Father's Off Inventions

I bet you my dad would have mistrusted
the steam engine when it first came in,
or Mr Bell's telephone; Mr Baird's television.

I remember he thought the fax
was a figment of my imagination.
What a scream.

I remember him freaking out
when he had to feed us at my aunt's house.
He went green when he saw the microwave.

He held the potatoes at arm's length,
then, panicking, threw them in,
shutting the door with a bang,

sent us children to sit in the garden
and wait for the noise *ting*.
I mean, imagine.

Once someone bought him an ansamachine
for his birthday and he burst into tears.
I had to leave the message.

Now, he said. *Hurry. Before the Bleep.*
All he wanted me to say was: *This is*
802 9 triple 3. I am sorry.

Then he crouched by the machine
for hours waiting for someone to ring.
There was me wanting to go iceskating.

'We can go out now. That's the whole point.'
I shouted, frustrated. *Just one message*, he said.
My dad won't move with the times.

He refuses to get a plastic hip
even though he's got arthritis
and he'd have a fit if he had to press

the pause button on the video.
Some people are just slow, slow.
'Leave me,' he says, 'off you go.'

Best Pal

I have stayed the night at Charmaine's
loads of times,
but she has never ever stayed at mine's.

I have asked her mother week upon week
no luck –
'maybe another day,' is all she'll say.

Last night Charmaine finally came.
In her bag,
a rubber sheet we spread on my bed.

Now I know Charmaine wets the bed,
we are close,
closer than before, close as sisters.

The Electronic Ladies

I went into a toilet, *uptown*,
turned round, put my hand out,
and the toilet flushed,
suddenly of its own volition.
I stared, scared.
And then I saw the red eye watching.

I put a hand under the tap
and the water gushed out
without me doing anything.
How come they know I'm here?
The Flush and Tap Spies.
And then I saw the red eye watching.

I put my hand under the drier,
all this hot air roared out.
I took my hand away,
it stopped. I put it back again,
it started. I was sweating.
And then I saw the red eye watching.

I want a flush I have to push,
a tap I have to turn.
I want a reliable paper towel.
Next thing it will be
an electronic bottom cleaner.
And then I'll see the red eye winking.

Harvey

My brother's best pal was his rabbit Harvey.
Harvey kicked his hind legs and peed
on anyone else who wasn't Maxie.

Harvey was an albino with bright red eyes.
Long grey ears. A nose constantly twitching.
Harvey didn't like his hutch. Much.

Once Harvey caught influenza
and came into our house. Maxie fed him
brandy out of an old eardrop bottle.

Harvey liked to munch the TV wires
watching the telly. Once, he gave himself a shock
so he went back to his bed of shredded News.

One morning Harvey was nowhere to be seen.
His hutch door was wide open, his cabbage uneaten.
We couldn't find him anywhere in the garden.

For three weeks we entertained possibilities:
maybe someone nice had built him a new hutch;
maybe he had fallen in love with another rabbit.

Harvey had been missing for twenty-two days
when Maxie came into the kitchen, a cabbage green,
saying, 'I've found him. I've found Harvey.'

He had been mowing the back garden when
he discovered Harvey near the rhododendrons,
half-buried, strangled, his neck lopsided.

For weeks I couldn't sleep for thinking
'Who would do such a thing?' as my bedroom
closed in, criss-crossed chicken wire.

The Gaelic Dog

(For Mabs)

refuses to speak English. She can walk all the way
from Kilmahog to Aberfeldy (through the Pass of
    Killiecrankie)
without speaking a single word of enemy
tongue. On return to Torridon, she
shuts the door, only if I say,
Duin an dorus. When I say, 'Walkie',
she tosses her long hair, fair scunnert. Aye.
Even turns the heid the ither way.
But if I say *Tiugainn* she positively
bounds and leaps and licks my feet; so many
kisses. She does a Highland dance with swords, high-
paws and barks in a breathtaking key,
the Gaelic for we're off to Tipperary:

Tir nan Og. Tir nan Og.
Who is a very happy dog?

But once the Gaelic dog did not eat for a week
because her mistress went away. Nor get any sleep.
Because the new woman said the wrong words. Eeek.
Biadh was food and not *Biadh*.
So the Gaelic dog pined in the corner like a sheep
about to be sheared; meek,
and sad and lonely, getting bony, slim as a leek,
dreaming the Gaelic dog dream of biting English
    feet.

37

Wild Goose Chase

In a furious mood one day,
I set off to get away
from my very annoying family.

I found myself at the bottom of a farm
where geese and lots of white swans
seemed to take a sudden

fancy to my sandwich.
(One especially) I didn't know which
way to run. I fell into a ditch.

Got up and the goose had the tail
of my brand new anorak well
in its beak, waving it like a sail.

I kept running. It kept running after.
I could hear the other geese's laughter.
My own shadow was a wild goose running faster.

Wish Wish Wish

I wish my mum didn't wear odd clothes.
I wish mine weren't secondhand.
I wish I didn't have such a big nose.
I wish I could escape to Neverland.

I wish my eyes didn't constantly blink.
I wish I didn't wear glasses.
I wish I did something other than think.
I wish I looked like other lassies.

I wish my voice didn't shake.
I wish my hands wouldn't sweat.
I wish my life wasn't full of mistakes.
I wish I didn't always forget.

I wish my freckles would move down my back.
I wish I had another name.
I wish I was popular and in a pack
of giggling girls, all the same.

I wish my hair was straight.
I wish my teeth were too.
I wish I could stay up very late.
I wish I was you.

The Want-Want Twins

We are the Want-Want Twins.
We go from shop to shop.
We are the Want-Want Twins.
We don't know how to stop.
One day it's a bow and arrow.
Another it's a dinosaur.
What are we going to get tomorrow?
More. More. More.

We are the Want-Want Twins.
Our eyes sharp shiny pins.
Our hands quick shark's fins.
We go from shop to shop.
One day it's the game Frustration.
We don't know what we need.
Another it is compensation.
Greed. Greed. Greed.

We are the Want-Want Twins.
We're completely over the top.
We are the Want-Want Twins.
We don't know how to stop.
We send our parents every night
A list that goes like this:
2 new bikes. Don't be tight.
x.x.x.

We are the Want-Want Twins.
Money grows on trees.
We are the Want-Want Twins.
We are the bee's knees.
All we want is everything.
We don't know how to stop.
We will be the Want-Want Twins till we
drop drop drop.

Corner Shop

Today, the corner shop is a car parts shop.
Before that it was empty for weeks
with a big white sign saying TO LET.
Before that it was a DIY.
But people got so good, they made their own tools.
Before that it had a big white sign saying TO LET.
Before that it was a florist run by identical twins,
who spoke the same words at the same time:
'The daffodils are an honest flower for spring.'
Before that it was a bakery run by a man
who wore a tall white hat and ate his own cakes.
Before that it was a Caribbean fish shop
run by a Trinidadian woman who showed you how to
clean the dead man's fingers from a crab,
or told you that bream tasted of trout.
Every day, when closing, she washed the floor
and all the water chased me to my door.
Before that it was a corner shop
selling everything – shoepolish sweets soup
soap salad salt shampoo spaghetti,
but only things beginning with S;
no tea no toffee no treacle no tomatoes.
'Nobody can survive in that corner shop,'
my mum says, weak smile at the new hopeful owner,
who is painting it for the umpteenth time
and putting up a brand-new sign.

Cracks

This morning

    on my way to school

        I had to be very very careful

mostly walk
       on tip toe

avoid streams, ignore spider's webs

watch
out   for the cracked egg
    and the geometric lines of an atlas

(HORIZONTAL V
                E
                R
                T
                I
                C
                A
                L radius.)
      All because

if I do, stand on a trench,

    a hairline
or a fractured bone,

I am in big trouble.

                                The minute
            I step
on a shattered frame, or a broken limb, I am out of
   line –
the cracked dragon, Bad Luck, will be on to me.

This minute.
YIKES.

I've had it.

Overheard Conversation on the Way to School

He's been picking on me for ages now and
I've been taking it. Well, I'm not taking
it any more, so there.

The thing is I've had to have a talk to myself.
Ask myself why this guy can try and make fun
of me and my country

and I just let him. Interesting question.
Well, not any more. He's had it with me.
Next time, I'm ready

watch me soar high above him, my big
angry wings flapping *do you think it's funny
do you think you're better?*

Up there in the air he will get smaller
and smaller until he is the size of a pigeon
dropping, a smudge, a blot

on the playground. I'm not hanging around,
hands on my ears, eyes close to tears, any
longer. Come on. Try me.

Everywhichway You Look (is someone who could steal me)

I actually had to say to my mother yesterday,
'Don't leave me sitting on the doorstep,
I might get nicked.' There's enough of it about.
You hear of children every day who disappear
in a split second or a blink of an eye.

Out shopping with my mother I am forced to say,
Don't bother with a basket. Put me in a trolley.
She doesn't take me seriously. *Baskets save money!*
The other day she was walking quick ahead of me,
in a bad temper. I said, 'You'll be sorry one day,'

running and sweating to keep up with her. I'm sure
there was a man in jogging pants running behind me.
He had red hair and a yellow jumper. I remember
things like this just in case I'm ever asked.
The way things are going I'm thinking my mother

is actually trying to get rid of me, bump me off,
make me disappear, *Why did I have you* she says,
or *Can I not have one single minute to myself*.
I have plenty time in my room when I'm lonely
to imagine her sad face when I suddenly die.

49

Sleekit

See after Sleekit falls asleep
she dreams a sleekit wee dream (the creep)
where she's at a busy birthday party, sniffs,
'Awful strange smell. Did you get a whiff?'

Smiles up her sleeve when Greta Green
tries to smell her oxters without Sleekit seeing.
In the morning, Sleekit wakes
to a clock set at a different time; six,

and when everyone else is rushing, mad
socks flying, shirts inside-out, she sits sad,
serene, doing a perfect figure of eight with her laces.
Her voice is North-sea oily; she pulls faces.

She goes to school to drive her pals mental.
Says, 'Ho, Jo. Get that dress in a jumble sale?'
Or offers a big bag of sweets, no joke,
then grabs your fingers in the bottom of her poke.

Sleekit spreads rumours like some people
spread bugs, chicken pox, or measles.
Says things that make you burn, your face hot.
'Once you tried to smother your brother in the cot.'

Sleekit creeps about the place
finding out things that put you in disgrace.
If I could get my hands on Sleekit, I'd dance.
But she's all slither, slide and slip. No chance.

Sleekit copies Gillian's answer on the war,
says, 'Oh look, we got the same again, *gold star*.'
But see when Sleekit
is discovered for her cunning wit,

Her skin glossy with gossip,
her sly, slinky, smooth ways; her lip.
What does she do first?
Blame it on Greta, Jimmy, Jo, Gillian, or worse,

her tiny toty wee sister (shame)
who screams in a big voice for a wee wean:
WISNAE ME WISNAE ME WIS HER AGAIN
WISNAE ME WISNAE ME WIS HER AGAIN

oxter – armpit

Runcible Spoon

(For Sue Dymoke)

And once in a different country
your father made you a spoon costume
for a school play. Such shining silver
wings could have flown you home.

And once the boys stopped you,
took the spoon and called you names,
till your terrified face shone
on the ground as they jumped on your reflection.

Your father's spoon, like the Welsh love spoon,
the Irish claddah ring; his way of saying
the feelings unsaid by his tongue:
a costume, a beautiful elaborate Runcible spoon.

Now, the big boys jumping, jumping.
Now, on your father's wide wide grin.
The one he made when he finished the spoon.
The wide grin that spanned a bird's wings.

On that flying smile the boys were jumping,
until you said *No*. No, like you were laying
an egg, a massive marble egg, freckled.
Nooooooooooooooooo. You became a fairytale.

And the boys, horrified, at this huge egg
in the middle of their street, stopped
calling your names, gave you back your silver spoon
and you, dignified, graceful, carried it home.

Dracula

After we'd climbed the many roads from Efori Nord
by bus past Bucharest, the capital of Romania,
I was dog tired. We went to a mountain room of pine,

and I searched the cupboards before I fell asleep.
That night I heard this weird flapping
at the window and woke up scared to death.

There, on the verandah, was a figure in black.
Casting no shadow. My hand instinctively flew
to my neck. Count Dracula was born here.

The cotton sheets were soaking with my sweat.
I could see his eyes flashing as he bent down;
imagine the two small sinister holes in my skin.

If only we had stayed in Efori Nord,
playing ping pong till Kingdom come.
If only we hadn't come to the mountains.

I crawled along the pine floor to my father's bed.
It was empty. Just a white pillow and a headrest.
My dad gave a loud guffaw from the balcony.

Took off his black cape; threw back his head,
said, 'Got you going there, didn't I?
Okay. The joke's over. Back to your bed.'

Can you believe that? All I am asking is:
who needs an imagination, a fear, or a dread,
when what we've got is parents instead?

Wee Red Van

My brother and I are staying with my gran.
My brother is eight, and a lot of bother.
I am six and my gran is sixty-eight.
I like to talk a lot. My brother doesn't.
And my gran likes *quiet*.

Today I just can't stop talking,
telling them a true story I find funny,
about *Kipper*, the teacher, who gets put in the sack,
for belting Lisa and breaking her pinky finger.
My brother says, *Not listening*; covers his ears.

My gran says, 'I'm warning you.
Quiet! Or it's the wee red van for you.
It takes mad children away and there they stay.'
So Kipper. . . . 'Right,' Gran says, 'That does it.'
But I can't be quiet. She gets up,

ties her scarf under her chin, a firm knot,
says to my brother, *I'm away for the wee red van.*
You watch her. And he says, 'Yes, Gran.'
I can't believe it. She actually goes out the door.
I watch her, two floors up, head for the red box.

My grandmother has gone to fetch the wolf.
I beg my brother to save me from its teeth.
He shrugs his shoulders, *'What can I do?'*
I visualize the inside of the wee red van.
The children won't talk, they will howl.

Ages later Gran returns, two hoods of chips.
Salt. Vinegar. 'That's you taught.'
I sniff and sob and eat my chips.
I can still see it. How they tied my hands,
and shoved me in beside the Alsatian.

Will I get over it? I don't see how I ever can.

Reddrick

Today was Reddrick's birthday. Three already.
Only Reddrick no longer lives with me.
Reddrick lives at the end of the road with the
  Murrays.

I went along there to see if I could wish her the
  best.
To my great horror she was outside, covered in rust.
No saddle; holes of decay along her bars; trust,

for Reddrick, a thing of the past. When she was
  mine
there wasn't a single chip in her colour, red wine.
I could see my reflection in her hands.

'Reddrick,' I whispered through the Murrays' gate.
She didn't even raise her head. I was too late.
She didn't even manage a very weak or irate

'Hello, how have you been since I last saw you?'
Though I could tell she heard me through and
  through.
Right down to her **one** pedal. 'Reddrick. I love
  you.'

I went home and cried for an hour and a quarter.
Then I went downstairs to give my mother what for.
I started quite casually: 'You'll never guess who I
  saw

yesterday, Reddrick!' But my mum was hardly
  listening.
'Reddrick, my old bike, you gave to Anne Murray.
  Sickening
state she was in.' *Uh huh* my mum said, then back
  to reading.

I was so angry. I grabbed the paper and tore it in two.
'One day I just came home and Reddrick was gone.
  You
just gave her to the *poor Murrays* without asking. How

could you?' My mum was stunned. 'You didn't
  cycle any more, dear.'
'We didn't cycle. We talked.' I screamed and
  walked off. No fear.
She was wrong. Another birthday ruined. On to
  next year.

Car Wash

Before it starts, she winds the window
up, fast enough to panic the glass.
A dramatic pause. Then the water
makes its loud music before
the big dancers begin their ballroom
spins. Done up to the nines,
in fancy red and yellow skirts.
We can't tell if they are
moving us or we are moving them.
Before we can say Tango or Rumba
they're on the roof, dancing a frantic
pas de bas pas de bas pas de bas.
My mum utters a manic
TWO THREE FOUR. We are about
to be swallowed up in their skirts.
All that terrible taffeta.
I go ga ga, shout Duck, Duck.

All of a sudden,
they just stop dancing.
Not even a feeble wee pas de double. Nothing.
Just stand back with their arms in the air.
Their hair full of electricity.
A green light flashes – GO – – GO –
But we still haven't gone.
We've been here a week.
I go out to the station to get us odd
things to eat, but I've had it with Hulas
and barbecued beef. I want home.
My mum's actually clutching the wheel.
Says she's got no power in her elbow.
Doesn't like the look of the flashing – GO –
'Don't be daft, mother. Let's GO.'
'No, no, no,' she says, and turns on the radio.

Good Food Guide

I wouldn't touch a hamburger
but I crave guacamole,
gazpacho and water melon.
I wouldn't go near fried bread,
but I would go bananas
for a blueberry pancake.
A glass of milk tastes very sly,
but sweet lassi would go down nicely.

There's things I wouldn't consider:
an English breakfast with ketchup.
But I'd stand up and shout
please, or go down on my knees
for ackee and cornbread,
baba ghanoush, ratatouille,
couscous, tagliatelle.
Don't give me custard and jelly,
give me sweet potato pie,
or tiramisu or Turkish delight.

There are words that taste
better than chocolate
words that roll and melt
words that can dip and swirl and sigh
words that make my mouth water
words that I can relish and suck and savour.

Go for the tasty, delicious words –
sag aloo, gadoh gadoh.
Don't give me a boring old plum.
Try me with a dim sum.
I'll eat my words.

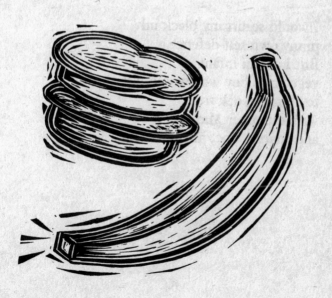

Maxie from Mango Class

did this to me,
split my lips into a burst plum.
He pushed my head into the climbing frame.
He is a meat-eater, not a Junior.
I am Maxie from Oak Tree,
a vegetarian eater
with bleeding lips.

Maxie from Mango class
did this to me,
gave me two big shiners for eyes, damsons.
My heart is heavy as a water melon.
I'm fed up with fighting,
the taste of bitter lemon.
If I was an octopus,

I would squirt my black ink
in my own self-defence.
But I am an infant
vegetarian boy who would like
to climb an oak tree
with the other Maxie
and share a ripe, juicy mango.

Girl Bully

I used to be a bully.
I did things like
if Fiona Harvey had something I liked
(a brand-new bike) I'd make sure
nobody talked to her, not even
when she tried to offer *free rides*
(get that). Twat. 'Nobody wants a shot
on your stupid bike. Anyway your saddle
smells.' I sat on my high horse
and threw evil looks at any girl who wavered.

Sometimes, I'd get my gang ready,
so when Fiona Harvey walked by
in her pathetic new trainers,
we'd shout *HEY BIG SPENDER*.
Othertimes, I'd get bored with Fiona.
She never cried or put up a fist.
I'd turn on Elspeth Mackintosh,
who was getting on my nerves
with her, *yes Lisa, yes Lisa, yes*.
'Elspeth will never have a bra will she?'
I'd say and ride off on Fiona's chopper.

Once I went to Elspeth's house after
I'd banished her from *Girlgang*.
Nobody else would come; I went alone.
Two wet eyes behind the letterbox.
The door opens two inches.
Elspeth's father yanks me into the hall.
'You've got a nerve on you, girl.
Turning up here to rub salt in it.

If you were my daughter,
I'd give you what for Hell.'
He shook me. Her mother poked me:
'How come' – her mother spits,
like fat in a chip pan –
'how come You, girl, are never alone?'
I handed Elspeth's white scarf back,
then did something I never do:
I said, *sorry*. I started to cry.
Elspeth's eyes gleamed Victory.

Kimberley

The kids at my primary school were all white
and no one ever called them *whitey*.
They used to shout things like *Kunta
Kinte*, *Kunta Kinte* running after me.
If I was with a friend crossing the burn,
I found these names even more embarrassing.
My friend could watch my cheeks burning.

But one day, a new girl arrived from Hong Kong.
Kimberley Lee. I was eleven and so was she.
The children in the playground descended
on her as if she was good prey;
vultures swooping down with *Chinky
Chinky*, *Yellow face*, *Slanty eyes*.
I watched the names bruise on Kimberley's skin,

full of pity and of relief —
which made me feel I was full of sin.
And once I tried the terrible name myself.
Chinky. I felt the word sizzle on my tongue.
That night I couldn't sleep for guilt.
And the next day I was full of sorrow.
I tried a new word out. S-sorry.

Betrayed

Kathleen Baxter went off with Audrey Smythe
I stared at the walls of the playground.
Audrey had a nice long pony but a plain face
I couldn't understand what Kathleen saw in her.

It was me who kept quiet about her diarrhoea.
Visited her every day of her gastroenteritis.
What had I done? It made me sick to look at them,
hand in hand, going to the swimming baths,

whilst I tagged behind with Wendy MacTavish,
of MacTavish chippie, who smelt badly of fish.
I'd watch Kathy and Audrey in our old corner
whispering viciously. What about? Me?

At home I'd pretend to my diary Kathy and I
were still best friends, and write down our day.
Then my mind would wander off to a special look
I saw earlier, being passed between Kathy and
   Audrey

like a tiny dazzling silver ball, thrown and caught.
Those little smiles made me want to throw up.
   Yuck.
Ill, I took to bed. No one brought me *anything*.
'Dear Diary,' I wrote, 'K came to visit today

brought a beautiful big bouquet.
She's worried to death I'm dying.'
So am I. I'm sure I am. That dreadful
disease, what's-its-name? I have the symptoms.

Names

Today my best pal, *my number one*,
called me a *dirty darkie*,
when I wouldn't give her a sweetie.
I said, softly, 'I would never believe
you of all people, Char Hardy,
would say that word to me.
Others, yes, the ones
that are stupid and ignorant,
and don't know better, but
not you, Char Hardy, not you.
I thought I could trust you.
I thought you were different.
But I must have been mistaken.'

Char went a very strange colour.
Said a most peculiar, 'Sorry',
as if she was swallowing her voice.
Grabbed me, hugged me, begged me
to forgive her. She was crying.
I didn't mean it. I didn't mean it.
I felt the playground sink. *Sorry. Sorry.*
A see-saw rocked, crazy, all by itself.
An orange swing swung high on its own.
My voice was hard as a steel frame:
'Well then, what exactly did you mean?'

Amber and Chocolate

(*For West Bridgford School*)

I am in love with Amber, right,
dead passionate like, like
nothing that's ever happened.
See me, I'm saft in the heid –
I just need wan look at her
and ma heart goes putty,
like a broken windae, like
the inside of a golf baw
when it's pulled apart. See me,
I'm that string, that scrambled
elastic. I'm a wobbly thing.
I tip-toe through life wishing.
See the things I wish, they're
mental. Bar L. The boys
say: 'Jamez, Jamez has got
a screw loose.' The boys
said that yesterday. Whit
a day. I went to the big
bit of bother of baking Amber
a special birthday cake.
Death by chocolate. Whit
a name, I even bought cawndles.
And lit them. All thirteen.
I had tae buy a six inch high
baking tin frae ma pocket lolly.
That's me fir the week. Nae sweets.
Nae comics. I wis deflatit

when my sponge collapsed
and I had tae pit the cawndles
in the sunken hole in the middle.
The things you do for love.
A big dirty chocolate cake. Blobs
of icing. I shot them on wey
wan of they guns. Bangbang.
Tried tae write *Amber* but
it came oot wrang. Anyhow.
Do you ken whit Amber says.
Naw. I couldnae credit it.
See me, I wis devastatit.
I haunded her the cake,
the wee cawndles flickering
like my ain heart and me singing
(off key) the Stevie Wonder version
of Happy Birthday and she says,
Amber says: *I don't like chocolate.*

Divorce

I did not promise
to stay with you till death us do part, or
anything like that,
so part I must, and quickly. There are things
I cannot suffer
any longer: Mother, you have never, ever, said
a kind word
or a thank you for all the tedious chores I have done;
Father, your breath
smells like a camel's and gives me the hump;
all you ever say is:
'Are you off in the cream puff, Lady Muck?'
In this day and age?
I would be better off in an orphanage.

I want a divorce.
There are parents in the world whose faces turn
up to the light
who speak in the soft murmur of rivers
and never shout.
There are parents who stroke their children's cheeks
in the dead night
and sing in the colourful voices of rainbows,
red to blue.
These parents are not you. I never chose you.
You are rough and wild,
I don't want to be your child. All you do is shout
and that's not right.
I will file for divorce in the morning at first light.

Attention Seeking

I'm needing attention.
I know I'm needing attention
because I hear people say it.
People that know these things.
I'm needing attention,
so what I'll do is steal something.
I know I'll steal something
because that is what I do
when I'm needing attention.
Or else I'll mess up my sister's room,
throw all her clothes on to the floor,
put her gerbil under her pillow
and lay a trap above the door (terrible)
a big heavy dictionary to drop on her
when she comes through. (Swot.)
This is the kind of thing I do

when I'm needing attention.
But I'm never boring.
I always think up new things.
Attention has lots of colours
and tunes. And lots of punishments.
For attention you can get detention.
Extra homework. Extra housework.
All sorts of things. Although
yesterday I heard the woman say
that I was just needing
someone to listen. My dad went mad.
'Listen to him!' he said. 'Listen!
You've got to be joking.'
Mind you, that was right after
I stole his car keys and drove
his car straight into the wall.
I wasn't hurt, but I'm still
needing quite a lot of attention.

Three Has Gone

'Yes,' Matthew said to
me, sadly, thoughtful,
'but three has gone now.'

'I don't want to die,'
I told them on my third birthday
'No way.'

'But you won't die,
until you are an old man, probably,'
they told me.

'I don't want to die even then.
I don't want to hold my breath
in for that long. Imagine –

down under the ground, gulping a breath
that will last a deathtime,
holding it longer than a swimmer

underwater, keeping my face straight
summer through to winter, looking so serious,
my lips pursed so tight,

you'd think I'd just told a huge lie.
No, I don't want to die.
It would be too tiring, expiring.

Death is holding your breath.'
I said that when I was three,
but three has gone now.